THE flourish colouring Book

Art Therapy Mindfulness

An empowering & relaxing palette of colouring art therapy for grown-ups, with flourishing tips, inspirational quotes & affirmations

Words by
Cheryl Rickman

Illustrations by
Amy Harwood

INTRODUCTION

About this book

Colouring-in has become a preferred winding-down, mellowing-out, de-stressing activity for grown-ups. Colouring-in is therapeutic and relaxing, but it also stimulates that innate creativity within us which adulthood, jam-packed schedules and responsibilities can tend to squish.

Simultaneously, mindfulness has become an increasingly well-known tool. Mindfulness can bring busy, stressed and/or depressed people back - from an anxious world filled with judgements and worries - to the present moment where they can focus on their breathing and be mindful about what they are currently seeing, hearing, feeling, tasting, and smelling… slowing down to be present and aware of the here and now.

Colouring is a useful tool in the mindfulness toolkit as it allows us to focus on the task at hand – shading one area and then the next – giving us the chance to take a therapeutic meditative art break. Because, when you colour in, the creative part of the brain is activated, whilst the information-processing part reboots.

Notably, the number of colouring books made specifically for grown-ups has grown exponentially in the past 12 months. At Flourish, we wanted to give you something extra; we wanted to provide a tool that, along with pages of beautiful illustrations to colour-in, provides helpful actions and easy strategies to enable you to flourish and make the most of this, your one and only life.

So, combined with inspirational quotes and encouraging affirmations, this is the ultimate colouring therapy book. Its pages will leave you feeling, not just calm and relaxed, but uplifted, empowered and equipped to take on all that is thrown your way, so that you may flourish.

About the Authors

Through her projects – Flourish and ClimbingTreesKids.com, and via the books she authors and ghostwrites at writer.uk.com – Cheryl Rickman wants to enable people to flourish in life, in childhood and at work. This mission, to help make the world a little less frowny and a lot more appreciative, positive and resilient, led her to collaborate with designer and illustrator, Amy Harwood to create a colouring book for grown-ups; one which provides the perfect blend of beautiful art therapy mindfulness, practical tips on how to flourish, empowering affirmations and inspirational quotes. The result is a beautiful blend of creativity-inducing inspiration and life-enhancing information.

Meanwhile, Amy Harwood's freelance illustration and design work has ranged from picture books and fashion graphics to Point Of Sale Design and branding, having worked with a number of brands from Debenhams and Next to Climbing Trees Clothing and Penguin. She also loves creating bespoke stationery and prints.

www.CherylRickman.co.uk
www.AmyHarwood.com
www.FlourishHandbook.com

What is Flourishing?

FLOURISHING is about more than simply feeling good, because, let's face it: happiness is just a fleeting feeling. Flourishing meanwhile, is about optimising well-being and achieving a more sustainable level of happiness which has staying power.

Based on a combination of the best-practice pillars of well-being (from the work of well-being experts, psychologists and authors, Martin Seligman, Emiliya Zhivotovskaya and Cheryl Rickman), there are 7 steps to flourishing. If we strive to use these areas as a checklist for sustainable happiness (which is essentially all that well-being is – happiness, but long-lasting)… we can live our best possible lives, maintain a high base point of well-being, accept and respond to adversity and thrive.

Step 1: MAXIMISING POSITIVE EMOTION
Step 2: MINIMISING NEGATIVE EMOTION
Step 3: HEALTH & VITALITY
Step 4: MEANING & PURPOSE
Step 5: SUPPORTIVE RELATIONSHIPS
Step 6: ENGAGEMENT
Step 7: ACHIEVEMENT

How To Use This Book

Flourishing Step-By-Step Pages

There are 12 months worth of tips and tasks to enable you to flourish step-by-step, based on the core pillars of well-being. The best way to ensure that you implement these quick and easy strategies into your life is to jot them down into your diary/pop them onto your calendar (e.g. 'gratitude walk' or 'play' and so forth) or take a photo of that page so you carry it with you and refer to it during that month.

Colouring Pages

The colouring pages include quotes and affirmations which will also inspire, motivate and empower you in your journey. Together, by completing the monthly actions and colouring-in the encouraging words, you will be well-placed to embrace possibilities and flourish. (Ooh, and you'll be feeling more relaxed too)!

Step 1

MAXIMISING POSITIVE EMOTION

Regular positive emotion bolsters resilience reserves, boosts the immune system and has a number of other benefits which extend above and beyond happiness. This means that, the more positive emotion we feel over the course of time, the more able and likely we are to bounce back during times of adversity. Handy!

Positive emotions include JOY, GRATITUDE, SERENITY, INTEREST, HOPE, PRIDE, AMUSEMENT, INSPIRATION, AWE and LOVE. So, this month, let's do what we can to spark these.

Get Grateful
To Flourish This Month:

- Unlock positivity by focusing on what you DO have rather than what you DON'T have. Ask yourself:

    1. What is going right for me currently?
    2. What can I celebrate about today, this week and this month?
    3. What am I truly thankful for?

    Jot down three things you are grateful for every day this month. Practising and feeling gratitude has been scientifically proven to be one of the best ways to boost well-being. It really works.

- Reframe. When you're feeling overwhelmed or stressed about all the things you've 'got to' do, try replacing 'I've got to...' with 'I get to...'.

  For example... 'Argh, I'm so busy but now I've got to go to my daughter's assembly'. How about reframing this to say, 'I get to go to my daughter's assembly. Not all parents can get the time off work to do this. It's a privilege to get to do that. And for that I am grateful!'

- Devote half an hour each weekend to looking through old photographs or videos and reminiscing on good times. Dr Seuss wisely said: "Sometimes you will never know the value of something, until it becomes a memory." In life, we have three chances to optimise each moment.

  1. Anticipating a happy event
  2. Savouring and enjoying it as it happens
  3. Expressing and recalling that happy memory

In doing all three we can **amplify** that magical moment.

So this activity, not only gives us a chance to relive special moments and recount the good feelings associated with them; it reminds us to anticipate and savour those moments before they occur and whilst they are happening.

Notice, Embrace, Connect With Nature

To Flourish This Month:

- Find a place where you can see a huge expanse of sky and/or water (ocean/river or stream). Go and sit there and get awe-inspired by the majesty of nature. Listen to the sounds around you. Soak them up. Breathe out worry and breathe in serenity.

- Go for a 15-30 minute walk through woodland or along country lanes, near a river or through your local park – anywhere that trees exist. The Japanese call this 'forest bathing' as trees release stress-busting oils. As you walk, say 'thank you' in your mind for all that you are thankful for. Regular gratitude walks provide the multiple health benefits associated with walking, releasing feel-good chemicals such as oxytocin. Plus, they give you the opportunity to get some thinking time amongst nature in the fresh air. There really is no better way to start or end the day than a good walk in nature feeling gratitude.

- Find a place amongst nature to meditate. You can take your phone and find guided meditations on **Insight Timer** and **Soundcloud**. We recommend **The Pause** by This Epic Life's Kristoffer Carter. Focus on your breath and slow down.

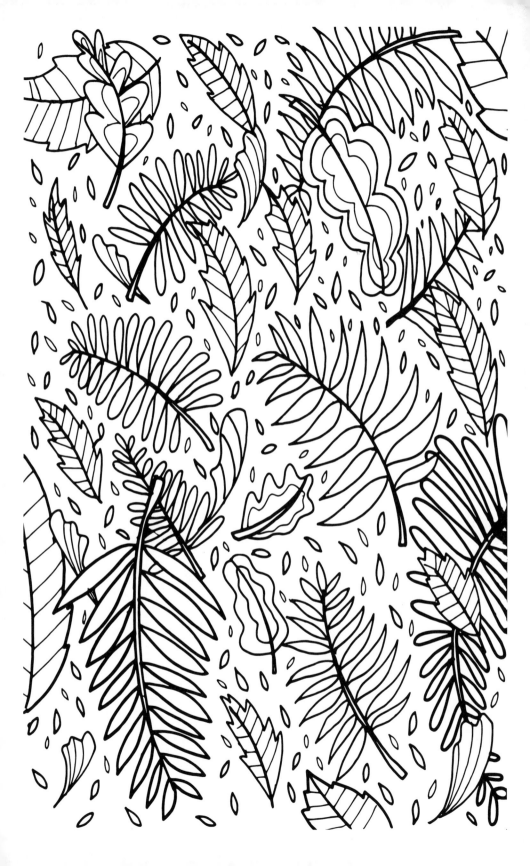

Create a Positivity Portfolio

To Flourish This Month:

Create a scrapbook, collage or mini photo-wallet of heart-felt moments (which is small enough to fit in your coat pocket or handbag or into a 'happy box'). You can use this to focus on the good and remind you about all that you have; to create instant positive emotion as it helps you remember, revisit and reconnect with a previous joyful memory/positive emotion. It should include:

- A photograph of your best friends.
- A photograph of you with your family (your 'us'/team).
- Words of praise you've received in your life.
- Your gratitude list listing 10 things that you are most truly thankful for.
- The first photograph of your child(ren)/nephew or niece when he/she/they were first born.
- A photograph of them laughing.
- A photograph of your pet(s).
- A photograph of a moment captured from a recent holiday.
- A symbolic beacon of hope that says 'You survived'.
- A symbol of pride in your achievements and/or your childrens' achievements (e.g. photo of your garden in full bloom, a medal you've won, front cover of your book, a photograph of your child swimming by themselves for the first time).
- These words jotted down on the back of your 'achievement symbol': "If I can do this... then I can do anything!" :-)
- Something that makes you laugh, e.g. a photo of your other half pulling a funny face or your favourite joke or one line summarising the last time you cracked up with laughter.

- A photo of your role model with a word that summarises why they're your role model (e.g. strong, kind, empowering, inspirational).
- An awe-inspiring image (e.g. sunset, nature in all its glory, an achievement such as Neil Armstrong's moon-landing or Jessica Ennis' medal win or similar).
- Happy images. Waves/beach/favourite book cover from your childhood.
- A photograph of you as a child. To remind you to be kind to yourself.
- Quotes, letters or other personal artefacts which connect you to feeling good.

Savour Moments. Savour Life.

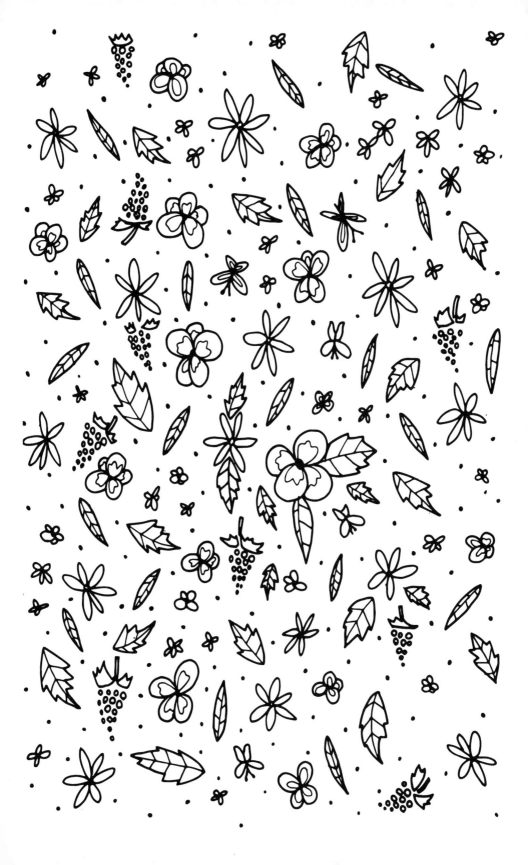

Step 2

MINIMISe NEGATIVE EMOTION

Negativity gets a bad press. Yet tough times can actually be useful times because, in coping with hardships we prove that we can handle it (remembering that when we are racked with anxiety and worry can be useful). Without the rough it'd be harder to appreciate the smooth. Ultimately, we are the sum of all of our experiences, both good and bad ones. And, if we got rid of all the sad stuff we wouldn't be us, nor would we be equipped to cope.

Sometimes we should accept feeling down; own it, release it (through crying) but then move on. Because it is the duration of negativity that doesn't serve us, rather than negativity itself.

Continuous negativity and dwelling prevents us from being open to possibilities. It depletes our positivity resources and makes us LESS RESILIENT. Conversely, positivity helps us to see the bigger picture and bolsters our resilience, so that we are better able to cope with all the crap that is flung our way. So, here are some ways to minimise the time you spend feeling bad.

Nip Negativity In The Bud
To Flourish This Month:

- List all the curve balls and adversity that you've been through and had zero control over. Was it tough? Yes. But did you get through it? As Helen Keller said, *"a happy life consists not in the absence, but in the mastery of hardships."* Those hardships can be helpful; they often teach us something positive about ourselves that we may not have known. Jot down what insight/opportunity those experiences taught/gave you that you didn't have before. Find the gifts in your hardships and hold your head high knowing that you can handle whatever life bungs your way.

- Diffuse your worries. We tend to default to negative perceptions of what might happen, but have no way of knowing what is yet to occur. So we just assume the worst. Instead, remind yourself that you can and will handle whatever you are worrying about. You did before (see above).

- Fact-check whenever a curve ball gets bunged your way and dispute judgements and put downs that your inner critic leads you to believe. List evidence to the contrary to counter those limiting beliefs and debate negative judgements that your inner critic is beating you up about. What's another way of looking at it? Your negative bias that worries, 'what if that happens' or warns you about your faults, has your best interests at heart. It thinks it's protecting you from harm due to ancient 'fight or flight' conditioning from when we needed warnings about what might happen in order to survive. But, often, those negative thought patterns have an adverse effect on your well-being and often warn you about imagined threats or overly-harsh judgements. Thoughts are not facts. But repetition of them does create neural pathways which become beliefs. These can be hard to shake, even when they are inaccurate. Thankfully, the more you talk back to your inner critic and dispute judgements and reassure your inner worrier, the more able you are to create new neural pathways and more accurate beliefs which better serve you. So practice.

- Turn off miserable media. Stop buying newspapers and watching the news (mostly bad) which you can often do nothing about. Watch inspirational TED talks instead.

I Can Choose my response

What often seems
the end of the world
often turns out to
be a positive and
transformative
experience

-Annie Lennox

Step 3

HEALTH and VITALITY

There's little point taking care of your mind without looking after your body too. You need energy in order to flourish, so your brain and body equally require plenty of scrummy nutrition. As such, it's important to focus on sleeping better, eating healthier and moving more.

Nourish Your Mind & Body To Flourish This Month:

- Schedule in at least three or four nights per week where you will get a good night's sleep. Switch off from technology an hour before bed; dim lights, write a 'to do list' to get as much as you can out of your head and onto a pad, mindfully feel how the duvet feels, the softness of your face on the pillow, focus breathing slowly in for five and out for five.

- Try progressive muscle relaxation to help you gradually release tension in each part of your body whilst you breathe in a controlled way. Start with your toes, deeply inhale through your nose as you flex your toes and hold the breath in for three seconds. Exhale through your mouth and relax your toes. Repeat with your legs, knees, hips, chest, hands, arms, shoulders... and snooze.

- Listen to meditation audio in bed. Fall asleep positively.

- Eat serotonin-inducing mood-boosting foods. Have a banana (or banana and blueberry pancake) for breakfast, seeds or almonds as a mid-morning snack; include pineapple, spinach, or cottage cheese in your lunch and turkey, bean sprouts, lobster, asparagus, kale, beetroots, or broccoli for tea. The nuts, seeds and green leafy veg will also boost your magnesium levels, which helps you to sleep deeper.

Step 4

MEANING and PURPOSE

Doing work that matters to you gives your life meaning and significance, and being significant is far more important than being successful. Living a purposeful life is a route to sustainable well-being, because it lights us up as individuals, but also helps us to make a difference in the world. As the legendary Scott Dinsmore of Live Your Legend so wisely said, "What is the work YOU can't NOT do? Go do it. Life's too short not to. The world would be an altogether different place if we all did work that mattered to us. Because, when we focus our time and talents on the work that means something to us, it starts to matter to those around us as well. That's what starts to change the world."

Find Your Forte and Live Your Purpose
To Flourish This Month:

- What would you do if you knew you might fail, but that didn't matter? What activities make you come alive? What do you just absolutely LOVE to do?

- Write down your strengths as you see them. What comes easily to you? What do others tend to ask you for help with? What are you best known for?

- Spend 15 minutes filling out this incredibly RIDICULOUSLY ACCURATE VIA Strengths Questionnaire designed by positive psychologists.
  authentichappiness.sas.upenn.edu/aiesec/Register.aspx

- Share your strengths and expertise. Teach someone to do something they cannot yet do. Teach children to cook, join a community gardening programme and teach others. Helping others to achieve what you are hoping to achieve can give your goals and daily life more meaning.

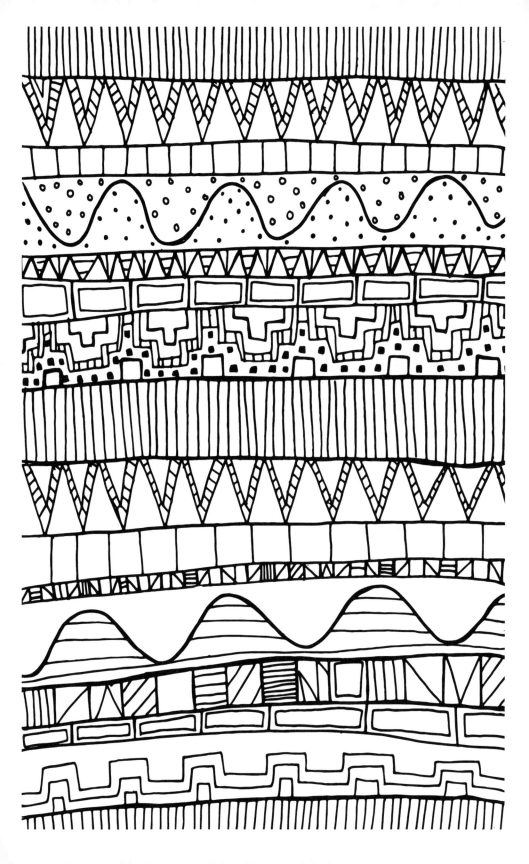

Step 5

SUPPORTIVE RELATIONSHIPS

Positive supportive relationships with other people contributes massively to our level of well-being. Having someone (or something) who is always pleased to see you and who you are always pleased to see is a vital contributor to happiness, as is having people to rely on for emotional support. People contribute to our best and worst times, our happiest and most painful moments.

Connect With Your Support Network To Flourish This Month:

- Buy some nice stationery or cookies or chocs. Write notes to people who support you. Send some thank you cards with flowers and edible gifts.

- Schedule in time this month to see all the people who make you feel good after spending with them. Make time.

- Ask people to share their good news with you. What's going well for them at the moment? Actively listen, ask them to relive those moments and show a real interest. Enjoy reliving those moments with them. Stay present and attentive to show your respect for what they are telling you.

- Designate one day per week as a Kindness Day. Volunteer for a local charity, donate blood, help an elderly neighbour with the shopping, bake cakes and give them away.

- Go out of your way to be kind at least five times this month. Get creative. Danny Wallace's 'Random Acts of Kindness' suggests: "Contradict demeaning graffiti (eg 'Andy Smells.' Write 'No, he does not.')" And "Buy some crisps from a vending machine and leave them in there." :-) Think creatively. What do those around you need most of all? Company, food, time, advice, a listening ear, your skills?

LISTEN MORE

Let us share our Experiences of falling and & CLIMBING & fALLING again. And getting back up again. ALWAYS.

Step 6

ENGAGEMENT

What you choose to spend your time doing and, more importantly, how you do it in terms of optimising your enjoyment of each and every experience, impacts your level of happiness.

Go With The Flow
To Flourish This Month:

- Revisit your youth. Do something you used to do as a kid. Ride a horse, fly a kite, go roller skating, read Charlie And The Chocolate Factory... do it. Either spontaneously(ish) so you actually do the activity today (or buy the relevant kite/ skates) or, if that is not at all practical, book it now. Put it in that bulging diary of yours. Schedule in your horse-riding kite-flying roller-disco day :-) Either do it on your own, with family or invite friends. Then play so much that you lose track of time and experience an engaging sense of flow.

- Step boldly outside of your comfort zone. Stimulate your life by being brave. Give yourself a nudge towards the unfamiliar. Challenge yourself to do something you wouldn't ordinarily do, something that stretches your own boundaries and limitations. This does three things — it invigorates and stimulates you, gives you the means to live in the moment/ appreciate the now and it kicks complacency into touch.

- Create engines of happiness for yourself, i.e. activities which stretch you at first, but then constantly stimulate you each time you add a log to the fire by doing them again. Schedule these mini-adventures into your calendar this month and beyond.

Advice from a tree

Stand tall and proud

Go out on a limb

Remember your roots

Drink plenty of water

Be content with your natural beauty

Enjoy the view

Step 7

ACHIEVEMENT

Just as *what* you do and *how* you do it are important, (to savour moments, make meaning, engage in your activities and consequently optimise each experience) *why* you do what you do is equally vital. If you pay attention to your intentions and ultimate vision for living your best life, you can create a meaningful action plan that'll help you to achieve goals that really matter to you, step-by-step towards your dreams.

See Your Future and Plot Your Route Step-By-Step To Flourish This Month:

- Consider where you are now on your life's journey map and where you aim to be. What is your intention? What are your hopes for the future? Close your eyes and visualise your intended life in your mind's-eye and spend some time focusing on it. View yourself showing someone around your dream house or taking your book off the bookshelf to show a friend. You did it! Look around you. What can you see? Sketch it out. Outline in your mind's eye your surroundings in every detail. How are you feeling? Who are you with? What are you saying? Imagine yourself telling them the story of how you got here. Raise a glass to your achievements, your friends, your family and feel complete and utter gratitude for what you have now that your dreams have come true. Feel the positive emotion within you. Smile. Take some deep breaths in and out and continue to look around you noticing all the details. Play it out like a showreel movie. Sit back and enjoy it.

- Open your eyes and write down affirmations based on that vision. For example, "I live in my dream home in this village. We often have friends over. The children love the garden, especially climbing the apple tree. My published books fill the shelves. Thank you for our happy home." Write all of this as if it has already happened.

- Find a pocket of time within your day or evening to visualise as regularly as you can. Before you go to sleep or whilst you're taking a shower can be good times to visualise. Anticipate all the possibilities and opportunities that await.

- Set your goals towards that vision. What do you hope to achieve en route to your destination? What needs to happen to bring that vision to fruition?

- Set your actions. Once you've set your goals you need to focus on them. What can you do each day to achieve your goal? What are the steps you need to take? Distil those goals down into bulleted action points – steps that you need to take in order to reach your destination, make your goals happen and get you where you want to be.

- Normalise your dreams by doing something today to live them out. For example, if you wish to climb a mountain, buy some mountain boots today... if you wish to travel to tropical climes, eat mangos and pineapples and create a vision board featuring images of those far-flung lands. Make your dreams more real.

what

does my

dream

look

like?

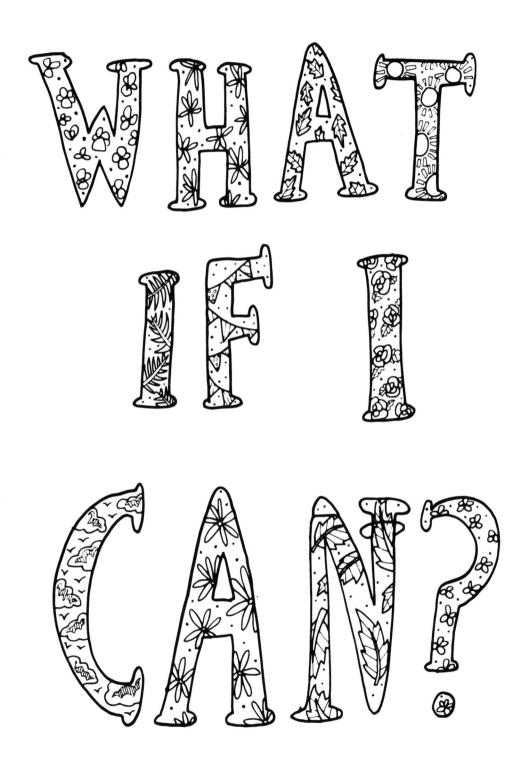

Made in the USA
Thornton, CO
07/18/22 17:11:03

6b54028c-863a-414c-8144-4644cc1a9582R01